JOHN'S LETTERS

LIVING IN THE LIGHT OF GOD'S LOVE

10 Publishing
a division of 10 of those.com

Copyright © 2017 by Peter Mead

First published in Great Britain in 2017

The right of Peter Mead to be identified as the Author of this Work has been asserted by him in accordance with the Copyright, Designs and Patents Act 1988.

British Library Cataloguing in Publication Data

A record for this book is available from the British Library

ISBN: 978-1-911272-42-7
Designed by Diane Warnes
Printed in the UK

10Publishing, a division of 10ofthose.com
Unit C, Tomlinson Road, Leyland, PR25 2DY, England
Email: info@10ofthose.com
Website: www.10ofthose.com

Peter Mead

31 UNDATED DEVOTIONS
THROUGH 1, 2 & 3 JOHN

 INTRODUCTION TO JOHN'S LETTERS

As John's Gospel comes to a close we read of John, Peter and five other disciples fishing on the Sea of Galilee when Jesus calls out to them from the shore (see John 21). Tenderly Jesus reminds His disciples of the time He originally called them to be fishers of men by repeating the miraculous catch of fish (see Luke 5:1–11). He reminds them of His continuing ability to provide through supplying another bread and fish meal by the Sea of Galilee (just like the feeding of the five thousand in John 6:1–15). He reminds Peter of his devastating denials of Christ by having another charcoal fire burning (see John 18:18). This poignant moment became a conversation where Peter, in front of the other disciples, was reinstated three times to a position of leadership in the flock of Christ's people. Fishing for men and feeding the flock – this was their commission as they followed the risen Christ.

But then Jesus spoke to Peter of how he would one day get to give his life for Christ, as he had longed to do before he denied his Lord so blatantly. At this point Peter and Jesus were walking along the beach, and Peter turned around and saw John. So Peter asked about John's future: 'Lord, what about him?' (John 21:20–21). Jesus' answer – 'If I want him to remain alive until I return, what is that to you?' – provoked confusion as rumours spread that John would not die, but that is not what Jesus had said. As it turned out, though, John did live for about three decades longer than the rest of the disciples. Most of them had been on the 'Peter path' – a path that led to martyrdom as they followed Christ. John was to walk the 'John path' – a path that led to death in his old age.

As we turn to John's three letters we are reading the words of an old man. He had been with Jesus, but about six decades passed by before he wrote the letters we have in our Bibles. In them he writes to believers in churches that he knew well. In the first letter John seems to be writing to believers that were hurting because some of their number had pulled out of the church with their own brand of super-spirituality that actually was not truly Christian at all. These departing ones had been very critical of those that remained.

So John writes with the wisdom of age and the authority of experience – specifically the experience of being with Jesus during His ministry years, His death and His resurrection. It is with that experience in view that John writes to comfort and encourage the flock of God. Let's turn to these special letters to experience that comfort and encouragement even today.

John launches his letter with a sentence crafted to invite his readers into the greatest privilege of all: fellowship with the Trinity!

He begins almost cryptically, diving in with a description of something very tangible. As awkward as the grammar feels, it does push us to notice the senses he is describing – hearing, seeing, touching. He and those with him heard it, saw it, observed it closely and even handled it for themselves. What is he referring to? Actually, the question is not what is he referring to, but who? He is writing about his experience of 'the Word of life' – that is, Jesus, the Christ.

Some people were struggling with the idea that the Son of God had actually taken on real, physical flesh. They were gripped by a false idea that the physical is a lower realm to be shunned, while the spiritual realm is what life is all about. John wanted them to know that Jesus really did come literally, physically – He could be touched.

John began his Gospel with a lot of the same ideas: 'In the beginning was the Word, and the Word was with God, and the Word was God ... The Word became flesh and made his dwelling among us. We have seen his glory, the glory of the One and Only, who came from the Father, full of grace and truth' (John 1:1, 14).

The writers of the New Testament books were eyewitnesses of something that really happened. It is easy for us, from a distance, to treat the Bible as if it is an ancient myth. But the Son of God actually came into this world, and what the Bible describes actually happened.

Here's the great news: Jesus did actually come, and really die, and literally rise from the dead; this means that **we can actually have eternal life, and really have fellowship with the Trinity, and literally enjoy life as it was intended to be enjoyed**.

REFLECTION

Ask God to reveal more of the wonder of fellowship with the Trinity during these days in 1 John.

As we've already seen, John wrote his letter to underline the great wonder of the Christian message: we can have fellowship with the Trinity.

John's ultimate goal is not to look back to the time of Jesus being on the earth, but rather to give assurance to the believers who would receive his letter in the present. In order to give assurance in the present, he had to look back to the fact of Jesus' coming into the world to be one of us.

The Son of God becoming one of us was a critical step in God's plan. There are many reasons why Jesus had to become a human, and we will explore more later. For now let's ponder just two of them:

1. To reveal the Father–Son relationship to us. Jesus is described as 'the Word of life' – He communicates the very nature of life itself. Since He reveals it, John and others can proclaim the message of eternal life. In John 17:3 Jesus Himself defined eternal life: 'that they may know you, the only true God, and Jesus Christ, whom you have sent'. If it weren't for God choosing to reveal Himself in His Son Jesus Christ, then we would not be able to know Him.

2. To share the Father–Son relationship with us. Jesus did not simply come on a revelation mission; He also came on a relational mission. God so loved the world that He gave us His Son. Jesus so loved the world that He gave us His relationship with His Father! In 1 John we will explore what it means to have relationship with the Father and His Son by the Spirit – that is, to have fellowship with the Trinity!

John was so thrilled by this good news that he wrote about it in order that he would have complete joy as his readers too came to share in what he was so enjoying. **The good news is so good it simply has to be given away.** And when it is, our joy will not diminish, but will only grow!

REFLECTION

If you struggle to give away the message of Jesus to others, think about the difference it would make to stop feeling pressured to proclaim the gospel, but instead to grow more and more thrilled with the gospel so that it overflows to others. Pray that this would be true for you.

The book of 1 John is known for being difficult to outline. The structure of the book is not easy to understand like Ephesians or Romans. However, in broad strokes, the book divides into two. First, John focuses on the truth that God is light (1:5 – 3:10). Second, he will focus on the truth that God is love (3:11 – 5:12).

John launches the first half of the book with a statement of this big thought: 'God is light; in him there is no darkness at all' (v. 5). John's opponents seem to have been denying that Jesus really came in the flesh, and therefore they would be relying on some other source of knowledge about God. But Jesus did come in the flesh and He brought a message about God – He is light without darkness; He is pure light.

The God you worship will shape the way you live your life. **If your God is light without darkness, then your life will be lived in the light**. On the other hand, as was the case with the false teachers, if you claim to have fellowship with Christ, but your life doesn't match up to that claim, you are being inconsistent. Thus John pointed out that the claim of the false teachers was a lie (v. 6).

However, his readers were 'walking in the light', in line with Christ's lifestyle. As a result, they had fellowship with one another, and they had their sins cleansed by the blood of Christ (v. 7).

In John 3:19–21, he had made it clear that there are two types of people in the world. There are those who believe in the light and move toward it. Also there are those who reject Christ and do not live by the truth. Why the latter? Because they love the darkness and hate the light. There is a consistency either way. So here in his letter John makes it clear that people may claim something, but that their lives will demonstrate the truth of that claim.

If people claim to know God, but their lives are dark and shadowy, then they do not really know God. For those of us who do truly know God, let's ponder the pure character of our God and ask Him if there is anything in our lives that is inconsistent with that.

REFLECTION

Ask God to shine the light of His character into your life and change whatever is inconsistent with who He is.

Yesterday we saw the first of three boasts by the false teachers: they claimed to have fellowship with God while actually walking in darkness. But they went further. They claimed that they were not guilty of sin! For John, this proved that they were deceiving themselves and did not have the truth in them (v. 8).

The truth is that we are all still living in a sinful world and we still have sinful impulses influencing our lives each day. But there is wonderful hope, even in this life. If we will cry out to God and confess our sins (instead of hiding them), then He will forgive our sins and cleanse us from all unrighteousness (v. 9).

According to John, God does this because He is both faithful and just. We might expect God to forgive us because He is merciful and kind, but John points instead to His faithfulness and justice. Why? Because he wants them to see the significance of Christ and His death. The false teachers were denying Jesus came in the flesh, but John wants the readers to think of exactly that. So he has pointed to the blood of Jesus in verse 7, and will point overtly to Jesus again after the next boast is refuted.

Here he subtly points to the cross and the death of Christ as a sacrifice for sins so that God is shown as faithful and just in forgiving those who confess to Him. God is faithful to His own plan in the death of Jesus as a just payment for sins.

In fact, John goes on to critique the boast of sinlessness further. Not only is this brag proving that the boaster does not have the truth in them and that the Word of God is absent in their life; they are also making God a liar. Why? Because God knows and states that we are sinners (v. 10).

God knows we will sin and thankfully He doesn't act as if we won't. God knew from the beginning that we would sin, so He provided Jesus to speak to the Father in our defence. It was God's good plan to send Jesus into the world to die and pay the penalty of my sin, even for the sins of the whole world!

REFLECTION

How amazing is it that God knows you will struggle with sin, and while He doesn't condone it, He does everything to deal with it! How good is the good news!

John writes with the heart of a loving pastor, and with the authority of one who knew Christ personally. (In fact, in his case, as the last remaining apostle, he knew Christ uniquely.) So he longs for the believers not to sin, but he writes with understanding that they will struggle with sin, as was made clear in 1:8.

John paints a beautiful picture for us. Next to the Father stands Jesus Christ the righteous, our advocate or representative. He Himself is the atoning sacrifice for sins. His sacrifice was good enough to pay for all sins, and it was made to pay for our sins.

The aged apostle wants to bring assurance to the believers – which he offers from verse 3: 'We know that we have come to know him if we obey his commands.' There is provision for sin. However, John knows that those who are in a personal relationship with Christ will not be defined by ongoing rebellion and sin.

Some will identify themselves with Christ, but their lives won't be marked by a growing Christlikeness. As we go on in 1 John, we will ponder how we become like the One we know relationally, like the person we love and like the One we look at. The first two of those three are seen here. If you know Christ and love God, then keeping His commands is not a totally foreign imposition on your life.

It is important to get the logic clear here in verses 5–6. The love of God enters a life and the Word of God comes in. That person, responding to the love of God for them, is then 'in him' and grows to become more like the God they know. Therefore they keep His Word and the love of God is 'made complete' or matured in them. **John is not saying that obedience leads to knowing God, but instead that knowing God leads to obedience**.

At this point it feels like there is a whole list of commandments to keep, but John will clarify what his commandment is in the next section.

REFLECTION

In what ways do you find yourself reversing 'I am loved, so I obey' into 'I obey to be loved'?

What if the commandments of God were to be summed up in one single command? What would that be? Jesus was asked essentially that question, and He answered with a single command expressed in two directions. We are to love – love God and love our neighbour (see, for example, Matt. 22:34–40).

Likewise, in his Gospel John wrote of that night when Jesus had washed His disciples' feet and then, after Judas Iscariot had gone out, gave them a new commandment. It was that they: 'Love one another. As I have loved you, so you must love one another' (John 13:34).

John was not giving any new commandment; he was merely repeating what Jesus had given to his followers back at the beginning. It was not new, but it might have felt new in the context of the challenges they were facing. They had seen their community of believers damaged by some false Christians who claimed to be in the light, but actually were in the darkness, and showed it by their lack of love for other believers.

John understood how Jesus polarised people. People were either in the light or in darkness as they responded to Jesus. They either loved or hated. There was no room for neutral apathy. So the false believers were not loving, but hating, because they were not in the light, but in darkness.

Jesus claimed to be the light of the world, and that anyone who followed Him would not walk in darkness, but have the light of life (John 8:12). **Jesus came to rescue us from darkness and death so we could join His Kingdom of light and life**.

In 1 John 2:11 John gives a key insight into the nature of darkness – it blinds eyes. That is, when someone is in the darkness, they typically don't know it. We see this back in John 3 where Jesus was approached by Nicodemus who wanted to talk about the things of God. But Jesus pushed back and essentially told him that he needed to be alive before that conversation could take place – he needed to be born from above. Nicodemus was spiritually dead, but he was convinced he was very much alive.

REFLECTION

Pray for God to shine his light into the lives of any in your church who are blinded by the darkness and don't know it. Pray that He will shine the light in areas of your life where the darkness may be clinging on.

In this section we find John addressing his readers as little children, fathers and young men. Throughout the letter he refers to the believers as little children, so the use here doesn't mean he is seeing the believers in three groups. Rather he is addressing everyone as his little children, and then he seems to be dividing the group between older and younger believers.

The whole set of statements offer great encouragement to the believers. All of them have their sins forgiven on account of the name of Jesus (v. 12), and therefore all of them know the Father (v. 13c). The gospel is so wonderful – the sins that separated us from God are dealt with and we are in relationship with God the Father. To know God the Father is eternal life (John 17:3).

To the older believers John simply writes that they 'have known him who is from the beginning' (vv. 13a, 14a). To know the One sent by the Father is eternal life (John 17:3).

To the younger believers John states that they 'have overcome the evil one' (v. 13b). When he comes back to them again, he gives more detail: they are strong and have the Word of God living in them (v. 14b).

When we put this encouraging section together, we have a description of a rich relational gospel. We have our sins forgiven because of Christ. We have Christ's Word dwelling in us, which strengthens us to overcome the enemy. And we know the Father and His Son, Jesus Christ.

The first half of John's epistle is really focused on the subject of living in the light that comes from the truth that 'God is light'. There is a huge emphasis on the moral impact of God's nature on the lives of true followers. Nevertheless, even in this section, **John is not allowing the reader to think that Christianity is merely a religion of morality and ethics; true life is found in relationship with the Trinity**. Holiness flows from that fellowship.

REFLECTION

Would you include yourself in the older or younger category? Does John's writing push you to ponder the privilege of knowing Christ, or of having God's Word abiding in you so that you can overcome the evil one?

Yesterday we saw that John was concerned with the need to overcome the evil one. Now he follows that with instruction not to love the world (cf. John 17:15–16). Later in this epistle he writes that 'the whole world is under the control of the evil one' (1 John 5:19).

His warning against loving the world is very strong – if anyone loves the world, then they don't have the love of the Father in them (v. 15). John then lists a summary of what is in the world. There are 'the lust of the flesh, the lust of the eyes and the pride of life' (v. 16, 2011 NIV). This sounds like the desire that drove Eve (and Adam) in Genesis 3:6: 'When the woman saw that the fruit of the tree was good for food and pleasing to the eye, and also desirable for gaining wisdom, she took some and ate it.'

We live in a time when the world is blatant in its tempting offers to draw us away from God. The lusts of the flesh are often portrayed in explicit sexuality. The lusts of the eyes dazzle us in a world of sensory overload. The pride of life is a constant draw as vanity seeks to seduce us through material possessions and positions of significance. 'Do not love the world or anything in the world' is a critical warning for us all.

But in John's context the warning is of something much more subtle. Often false teaching is not as blatant as the advertising around us. Those people who had left the church (also see v. 19) would have seemed religious and very 'Christian' in lots of ways. If they had simply rebelled and gone after gross sin, their true identity would have been more evident, and then those who remained wouldn't have needed assurance of their own salvation.

The desires of the flesh can be living life in one's own strength, apart from the life-giving Spirit. The desires of the eyes can be to live with physical sight rather than spiritual sight. The pride of life can be contentment with life as it is, leaving God at a distance. **It is possible to be very religious, but still really loving the world, when there is no true fellowship with God by His Spirit**.

REFLECTION

Where are you in danger of being seduced by the blatant temptations of a worldly culture? Where are you in danger of being seduced by the subtle temptations of a version of Christianity that is religious, but keeps God distant?

The world is a tempting place, but all its desires are passing away. What lasts is the will of God (v. 17). However, the believers John was writing to were struggling because something had not lasted. A group had gone out from among them and separated themselves.

The history of the church is littered with local squabbles and divisions. Sometimes these are caused by genuine doctrinal differences, other times by varying preferences over how church should operate, and often because of internal politics and the wrangling of power-hungry people. Division is always sad. But here John is clear that something even more sinister is involved.

He uses the end-times language of 'antichrist' to speak of the enemy of God in human form. In the Gospel of John we read references to 'the prince of this world' (John 12:31; 14:30; 16:11). There are times in history where the great adversary of God makes his presence felt in particularly human form. Down through the centuries others have used the same label to mark human figures opposing the church and the truth of the gospel.

We would be wise to avoid using this label too easily, but it would be naive to ignore the work of Satan in opposing the truth of the gospel. The group who had left the believers and gone out were not believers looking for slightly better worship music. They were denying the Trinity, denying the Son and undermining the reality of eternal life itself.

Satan is at work to draw people in the church away from the truth of the gospel. Satan does not want people enjoying the fellowship of the Trinity. Consequently he will work to shift our focus away from the relational nature of the Trinity, or from the truth of the Son becoming human to enable us to come into the fellowship of the Trinity, or from the gracious nature of the invitation to us. He would much rather we see God as distant and then focus on ourselves and our own efforts to be religious (which is almost always the nature of false religion).

How does John encourage the believers to stay spiritually safe? Not by engaging the enemy in some sort of spiritual combat, but by letting the message they heard abide in them. **As we stay in the Word and the Word stays in us, we are protected from the lies of the enemy**.

REFLECTION

How much are you letting the Word of God into your heart to protect you from the enemy?

 **DAY 10**

READ 1 John 2:20–21, 26–27

One of the most misunderstood ideas from 1 John is that if we have the Spirit, then we don't need anyone to teach us. If that is the case, why does the New Testament make so much of the gift of teaching and the role of the pastor-teacher in the life of the local church? As ever, understanding can only come as we recognise the message in context.

John is writing about a group who had gone out of the church denying the Trinity and the coming of the Son of God as a human. Since they denied the significance of the Son walking among us, they lost sight of both the moral implications of Jesus' life and the salvation that Jesus achieved by dying on the cross. John is clarifying that they were not true believers. Furthermore, the true believers, who therefore have the Spirit of God in them, do not need the supposed 'special teaching' of these false believers to access the truth.

It is worrying when people who seem to be very spiritual and knowledgeable start saying that you are the one who lacks something. It can be disconcerting to think that there is a 'super-Christianity' and I am on the outside of that category. But **John wants to reassure his readers that if there is a super-anything, they are the ones who have it**. Why? Because the anointing of the Spirit in this New Covenant age is for all believers, not just for a few. They have the privilege of having the Spirit. Just as the Son was anointed, He has also anointed them with His Spirit (see John 20:22), and as a result, they know God.

What is the role of the Spirit in the life of a believer? Paul wrote of the Spirit's role to be the love of God poured into our hearts (Rom. 5:5). Perhaps John's way of describing this sense of relational assurance is to see the role of the Spirit in bringing to mind all that Jesus had said to His disciples (John 14:26). Again, the work of the Spirit is intimately tied to the Word of Christ abiding in the life of the true believer.

REFLECTION

Give God thanks for good Bible teachers who point us to Christ. Pray for wisdom to discern when we or someone we love is drifting from the truth.

People are either children of God or children of the devil. And the family they belong to is demonstrated by the way they act.

John has just used the language of 'antichrist' that points to the end times. The bad news of this language also stirs the hope of the good news: that Christ is coming! So from John's perspective, there is a simple logic to the Christian life. We should abide in Christ now, resulting in both righteous living now and no shame when Christ returns. Those who do not abide in Christ will not live righteously.

How easily we get used to using astonishing language. For instance, we are children of God! John's Gospel introduced the idea of being born of God, and born from above by the Spirit (see John 1:12–13; 3:3–8). Jesus also challenged those who thought they were God's children – their behaviour demonstrated that they were actually children of the devil (John 8:42–47).

So John pauses to underline the wonder of being a Christian here in 1 John 3:1–3. First, he points to the kind of love that the Father has given to us. This is no grudging or conditional love. We are given the great privilege of being the children of God. The result of this is that the world will not know or understand us, any more than it understood or knew Jesus. The world's rejection of those who abide in Christ can be a source of reassurance for those who might naturally find this rejection painful and confusing.

Second, we have spiritual blessings now, but there is still more to come. The people who had left the community probably claimed they had everything already, so how they then lived didn't matter. John's readers already had the privilege of being God's children, but they also had a great hope. Their lives were changed by looking to Christ, and one day that transformation will be complete when they can gaze on Christ without hindrance or distance (see 2 Cor. 3:18).

Third, there is an implication here: such a hope in our future will stir a desire for purity in the present. How we live now does matter to us because Jesus matters to us. **Like a bride anticipating being with her bridegroom, so those who abide in Christ will care passionately about how they live as they prepare to see Christ face to face.**

REFLECTION

If a bride is passionately concerned about being ready for her wedding, how do you find your motivation for pure living stirred by Christ? Do you know Him well enough to stir such a passion for purity?

John was writing to comfort a group of believers. It is vital to remember his intent as we ponder his content. The danger, if we forget this, is that we may find this text profoundly discomforting!

The believers that John was writing to were being criticised by a group who had left the church to set up a rival, and supposedly superior, church community (as seen in 1 John 2:18–26). Yet these others were living lives marked by sin. John wanted to make it clear that there could be no correlation between greater spirituality and greater sinfulness.

Sin is a heart issue, but it often manifests in lawlessness. Jesus came into the world not only to pay for sin, but also to deal with sins in all their specific ugliness. Therefore someone who is changed by encountering Christ and by knowing Christ, indeed by being Christ's, will not continue to live a life marked by sin.

So does this mean that true Christians never sin? John has already established in 1:8 and 2:1 that believers should never expect sinless perfection in this life. What he is stating here is that being Christ's will make a marked difference in your life. The reason he can be so confident about the transformation that will occur in a believer, even though it will always be incomplete in this life, is because of his high view of the gospel.

The good news of Christianity is not simply that the death of Christ offers legal pardon for trusting sinners. That would be merely external. The good news of Christianity is internal too. Jesus died to pay for our sins, and also to purchase for us the privilege of new birth. That is, the Holy Spirit is the seed of God planted in the life of a believer. This internal reality brings a renewed heart and a change in desires. Also, the true believer abides in Christ (3:6, 9). We abide in Christ and He in us.

So we may struggle with sin, but we will not be characterised by it. The born-again believer, now a child of God, has the spiritual DNA of God within, thereby birthing the desire for a God-pleasing life.

Ongoing sin is a sign of a different paternity, because those who are not Christ's are the children of the devil. The devil seems to have the world in his grip, but there is hope. **Christ came to destroy the works of the devil and that destruction continues as one person after another is born of the Spirit of God into the family of God!**

REFLECTION

What sins manifest themselves in your life? How will fellowship with Christ continue the process of shaping a life that is not marked by sin?

At the midpoint of 1 John let's take a quick detour to John 8. Here we find Jesus in the midst of a tense interaction with the Jews, but it says many believed in Him. The next thing we see is Jesus pushing these so-called believers to the point where He identifies them as sinners whose father is the devil!

All the way through John's Gospel we find that not all belief is actually saving faith. That is, people can have a certain amount of belief in Jesus but not really be entrusting themselves to Him. Perhaps they just want His benefits, or perhaps they are just impressed by Him. But we find that Jesus is not satisfied by inadequate belief. **Someone can look like a follower of Jesus, but not be in relationship with Jesus.**

In John 8 Jesus raises two key issues. The first issue is the truth of the Word of Christ (vv. 31–41). If that Word finds a home in the follower, then that person knows the truth and is free. If the truth is not received, then that person remains a slave to sin and ultimately is hostile to Christ, the One who brings the truth to us.

The second issue Jesus raises is that of love (vv. 42–47). If the Word of Christ is received, then the Father of Christ becomes our Father and our response to Christ becomes one of love. Those who are not Christ's are not neutral. They remain children of the devil and do his desire, which is to hate Christ. There is a direct relationship between the truth of Christ and love for Christ.

So far in 1 John we have seen an emphasis on the truth. God is light and those who know Him will walk in the light. The truth will mark their morality. Now John is going to shift focus for the rest of the book to dwell on the issue of love. Many writers say that John's epistle circles through themes rather than following a linear progression. Certainly he has written about love already and will mention the truth again, but in the next days watch as he zeroes in on the love of God, indeed on the God who is love.

REFLECTION

Only God knows those who are genuinely His. It is not our place to be the judge. But consider how it can be both troubling and comforting that some who act like Christians actually are not.

Again, just like in 1:5, John introduces the message that they have heard from the beginning. This time his focus is not on God being light, but on the need for loving one another.

John begins with a bold counter-example. What does not loving one another look like? The Bible began with an immediate example of sin reigning in the human heart. After the perfection of Eden, the slide into sin was not gradual. Immediately after the Fall we read of Cain, who did not know or love God. Instead he hated because he belonged to the evil one. The result was not a little sin, but the murder of his own brother.

John tends to write in very black and white terms. He does not offer any shades of grey. People either love God or hate Him. People either love one another or hate one another. This seems harsh in a world so confused by mixed motivations and complex situations. Nevertheless, John cuts through all of that and offers us clarity in the midst of the mess.

For those who are children of God, who have been brought into the wonder of the New Covenant, this world is a hostile environment. The world is under the sway of the one who despises God's nature and therefore hate is the common currency. It may be couched, or disguised, or sugar-coated, but it is hate nonetheless.

John does not want his readers to misunderstand this stark context in which they live. Most of us tend to believe the best about any who label themselves as followers of Christ. But 1 John offers a warning and a comfort. It may be that we experience hatred from the world, just as Jesus warned His disciples (see John 15:18–25). And it may be that some in that hateful category like to dress up as followers of Christ. This is both a warning (it will happen) and a comfort (I've told you in advance).

But ultimately John is not offering mere warning or comfort. **John is giving an instruction: don't respond to hatred with hatred**. Don't go there. To do so would be to reveal that you also are on the other side.

REFLECTION

What is it about God that should stir us to love one another? What is it about us that stirs hatred in the world toward us?

It is all very well to write that we should love one another, but what does that look like? John has the ultimate example: 'Jesus Christ laid down his life for us' (v. 16).

Some people will read the story of Jesus going to the cross and see it as a horrible failure. Here was this wonderful teacher whose plans slid out of control and ended in death. That is not what the Bible so clearly teaches. Jesus came into the world with the intention of going to the cross. He set his face as a flint to go to Jerusalem. He never backed down, ran away, or protected himself. Jesus Christ laid down His life for us.

John writes that the cross is how we know what love is. But this is not just an explanation of love; it is also an example of love. **John expects believers in the love of Jesus to love like Jesus.** He starts with the ultimate expression of that love: we ought to lay down our lives for one another. And then he goes to a more practical everyday level: we ought to share what we have with those in need.

It is easy (in theory) to talk about dying for one another. Maybe if such a need arose, I would have my eyes on Christ and be able, by the strength He provides, to lay down my life for my brother or sister in Christ. But sadly I find it much more difficult to contemplate offering the lesser sacrifice of sharing my possessions with someone in need.

The cross of Christ calls us to entrust ourselves fully to the God who would give His Son to die for us at such great cost to Himself. The cross of Christ calls us to give of ourselves to others who are in need – whether they need us to die for them, or share our possessions with them.

It is easy to talk the talk of being representatives of the loving, giving God. John urges us to live out who God is by our actions.

REFLECTION

Take some moments to imagine what it was like for Jesus heading toward the cross – He laid down His life for us. Ask Him to stir your heart with love for others around you. Ask Him to show you how to love practically rather than merely talking about it.

Where should we look for assurance? After all, there will be others who try to make us doubt that we are secure in God's love. The enemy would certainly love to stir doubt in us. Sometimes even we seem to move ourselves into a place of doubt. So how can we find assurance?

John begins by pointing to our hearts and essentially states that we should not be trusting how we feel about our state of condemnation before God. For though we may feel condemned by our hearts, 'God is greater than our hearts, and he knows everything' (vv. 19–20), and He has proven His love for us by making us His children.

But John does not reject the importance of our feelings altogether. After all, the New Covenant involves a new heart and a heart-based awareness of God's law. So if we don't feel condemned, that is a source of confidence that we are now living in fellowship with God – asking and receiving, obeying and pleasing (vv. 21–22).

Then in verse 23 John offers a two-fold summary of the gospel that we obey. First, we believe in the name of God's Son, Jesus Christ. Second, we love one another as Jesus commanded us. We have already mentioned Jesus' two-fold summary when asked about the most important law – it is to love God and to love others (Matt. 22:34–40). So why does John make the first part belief in God's Son?

Loving God the Father is ultimately about receiving Jesus Christ, the Son who has forever delighted Him, and who He sent into the world because of His love for us. To welcome Jesus as sent from God is to be brought into that vertical dimension of love between God and humanity. Then, as a result, we become those who love others, spilling the love we have received to others. For John, true Christianity is not just a private commitment to God, nor is it just a human-level benevolence to others. It is really about being brought into the loving fellowship of the Trinity!

Consequently our assurance is not about ignoring our experience of God and looking to our behaviour, but rather it comes from the fellowship that we experience with God by means of the Holy Spirit who now lives in us.

REFLECTION

How do you sense the Spirit at work in you stirring love for God and others?

John has just stated that our assurance of being loved should come from the Spirit of God given to us. Obviously there is an implicit danger in this. After all, there is more than one spirit in the world. So how do we know that we are experiencing the Holy Spirit and not another spirit?

John urges the believers to test the spirits to see whether they are from God. The test is simple: the Holy Spirit will always celebrate Jesus according to the truth that He came from God in the flesh. But false spirits will always undermine the connection between the Son and the Father. Given that Satan launched his whole rebellion against God after watching the Father and Son in relationship, it makes sense that any false spirit will despise that connection within the Trinity (see Ezek. 28:11–19).

Once we understand the enemy's deep hatred of the bond between the Father and the Son, his destructive work starts to make sense to us. On the other hand the Holy Spirit could not be more thrilled by the love He communicates within the Trinity.

It is easy to feel threatened by the anti-Christ spirit that is at work in the world. The truth is that there is a great threat to us if we belong to Christ, but we need not fear. Why? Because verse 4 reminds believers that they are overcomers who have a greater God in them than the spirit that is let loose in the world.

Those working for the enemy will be influential in the world, but those who truly belong to God will have influence among those who truly belong to God's family. This means that we can test the spirits, and we can test which spirit people are influenced by. **The key issue is the fellowship of the Trinity: the Spirit of truth honours Jesus the Son sent by the Father; the spirit of error will always seek to undermine Jesus in some way.**

REFLECTION

Many of us live in an age where we assume there is very little influence by the spirits. The spiritual realm has been explained away. Prayerfully ponder how false spirits may be at work in your environment, and how the Holy Spirit is also at work in your life and in those who belong to God.

In 3:23 John gave a two-part summary of Christianity. The first part, believing in the name of Jesus, was developed in 4:1–6. Now, starting in verse 7, he is going to develop the second part of that summary: 'love one another'.

John urges the believers to love one another. Why? Because love comes from God. Those who are born of God are those whose lives will be marked by love. To know God is to love others. To not love others is to not know God, since love is so essential to who God is.

As we look to God to understand love, we get a glorious picture. God's love was made manifest among us because God gave His only Son so that we could live through Him. More than that, the source of love is not in us toward God, but in God giving His Son to be the atoning sacrifice for our sins.

When God sent the Son into the world, He was sending Him to come and die on the cross. It was God's plan all along. So we need not wonder what love is like; we can just look to God.

To say that God is love is to say something very significant about Him. As we ponder the nature of the Trinity, we find how intrinsic their mutual love is. Consider, for instance, the description of the Father's love-driven glory-giving in John 17:24. The Father loves the Son and the Son loves the Father, and the Spirit completes and communicates that love. At the core of who God is, we find love to be the bond.

If God is a self-giving and others-loving community of Father, Son and Spirit, then it fits that such a God would send His Son on a rescue mission, knowing what He would go through for our sakes. Jesus revealed the Father to us in His loving and self-sacrificing. It was not that the cross was just a necessary evil on the pathway to a preferred future. Rather, the cross is the place where the glorious love of God is revealed and proclaimed to the whole world.

REFLECTION

The cross is the place where we get to see God's character revealed most fully. In what ways do you struggle to see God as selfless and defined by His love?

What about the many of us who were not around to see the love of God presented on that hideous cross? John flows from the fact of God's love revealed in Christ to the overflow of that love as we love one another.

We are not limited to only describing the loving reality of a God in heaven who we have not seen. We also have the fact of the cross where that love was seen most vividly. And we have the opportunity to demonstrate God's love in our love for one another.

When Christians love one another, they don't simply paint a portrait of a historic love – as if the cross of Calvary has inspired a lingering effect in them. **The love of Christians for one another is an evidence of the abiding presence of the living and loving God in them, and a proclamation of the truth of God sending His Son to this world on His mission of love**.

Remember that John is writing to a group of genuine believers who were rocked by the departure of a group from within their church. That group spoke critically of them and spoke of their own superior spirituality. John is writing to reassure those remaining that they are not somehow on the outside of what God is doing in the world. The greatest assurance they have is that the Spirit of God has been given to them, as is evident in their love for one another.

The true Spirit from God is the One that points to the coming of the Son from the Father, and who does not detract in any way from the person and work of Christ. So John assures them that they are confessing rather than denying the truth about Jesus as the Son of God and the sent Saviour of the world. Also he assures them that they have the Spirit abiding in them – they have genuine fellowship with the Trinity.

To have fellowship with God, to have God dwelling in you and to be dwelling in God – by the Spirit, enabling you to worship Christ – is no second-class Christianity. This is the real deal.

REFLECTION

How does the Spirit of God point your heart to the wonder of who Christ is and what He has done? How does the love of God show up in your life as you interact with other Christians?

The true Christian loves God and God's people. It is simple, but it is so significant. This kind of love at work in and through us moves us toward maturity. A result of this is confidence in anticipation of standing before Christ's judgment.

This is not about anticipating Christ's judgment of whether people are saved or not – this is not what the Christian is looking forward to. Rather this is about that day when we will stand before the judgment seat of Christ to have our lives evaluated (see 2 Cor. 5:10). We don't fear that day. John has already referred to us having confidence when Christ comes back in 1 John 2:28.

How can we have confidence in antici-pation of an assessment from Christ? **We can have confidence before the ultimate evaluation because perfect love drives out any fear**. Fear is about anticipating punishment. But those who are united to Christ by the Spirit know that they are not going to be punished – God's love has dealt with that prospect.

Christian love is not something we work up within ourselves. We love because God first loved us. We love Him because of His love. We love each other because of His love.

Perfect love drives out all fear of punishment. To know we are safe and secure is an absolute treasure. We enjoy that kind of peace only in the most blessed of human relationships. If we have that with parents, a spouse, siblings, or friends, then we should be most thankful. In a fallen world there is fear interlaced with almost every relationship.

Just to make sure nobody tries to claim that they love God without loving their neighbour, John reiterates in verses 20–21 that these two 'loves' are intimately connected. If we love God, then we will love one another too. (And part of that will be the removal of fear from our relationships – we won't make people live in fear of our judgment over them. Our love for one another will reflect the love with which we were first loved by God Himself.)

REFLECTION

Think about standing before Christ at the end of your life. Does this fill you with any fear? Talk to Him about it. Thank Him for His love and let it continue to drive out that fear.

In this section John writes about some natural connections. To be a Christian is to trust in who Christ is and to love the Father who sent Him. To love the Father means to love those who are born of Him. To love the Father means to obey His commandments. This is all natural for the Christian.

This is a section of comfort for John's readers who were feeling the pressure of accusations that they were somehow inferior or less than complete Christians. However, we can easily read these verses and feel pressurised rather than comforted. After all, victory that overcomes the world sounds pretty impressive. But this passage is saying that such victory is the normal Christian experience.

To love other Christians, to obey God's commands and to have victory over the world seems to be a formidable trio of goals unattainable by normal people like us. Indeed these would be unattainable goals if we were left to our own strength. How can we love, obey and conquer by our own resources? Surely only a handful of super-saints could get close to this by their own efforts? But John is not describing a powerless gospel.

To trust in Christ is to be transformed from the inside out. In the gospel there is provision for profound transformation. **Not only do we have our sins forgiven (the record is wiped clean), but we also are given new hearts with a desire to please God (fleshy hearts with the law written on them in the place of stony hearts), and we are given the presence of the Holy Spirit uniting us to Christ.**

Consequently John can write as if the normal Christian life is marked by love for others, by victory over the world and by obedience to God's commands. That is why John can declare that God's commands are not burdensome or impossible. And that is why this passage is a comfort to the Christians he was writing to, rather than a pressurising exhortation.

REFLECTION

In what areas have you been striving in your own strength rather than finding your strength to love, obey and conquer in God Himself?

Before he finishes his letter, John wants to underline one more time who Jesus Christ is (since false teaching about Jesus was so prevalent in his day). He states that Jesus came by water and blood. Then he emphasises that it was not by water only, but by both water and blood.

How do we make sense of this? Perhaps the simplest explanation, and probably the right explanation, is that the water is referring to the baptism of Jesus with which His ministry was launched. Then the blood is referring to the crucifixion of Jesus which was the culmination of His mission.

There was the false idea that the Christ (a spirit) descended on Jesus at His baptism, but then left Him before His death. This idea allowed people to feel more comfortable if they believed that matter itself is inherently evil. It avoids having the Son of God actually walking around with human flesh. The main problem with this idea, and other variations, is that it is not true.

God the Son literally, physically and actually became a human. He was fully God, and He was fully human, and He was fully one. Jesus was still the Christ as He died on the cross. So the witnesses of the baptism and the crucifixion, and the Spirit Himself, all agree that this is who Jesus really is.

REFLECTION

It may not be Christmas, but take some time to think about God the Son truly becoming one of us and dying for us, and remaining one of us forever. Surely He is worthy of our worship?!

Christianity is about Christ. **It is not possible to diminish or dismiss the Son and somehow still have some connection to the Father**.

John presents two contrasting options. Option one is to accept what the Father has said concerning the Son. Back in John 5 Jesus stirred the anger of the Jewish leaders by making Himself equal with the Father. When Jesus started calling witnesses to support His defence, He stated that His key witness was actually His Father. Then He turned on the religious experts by telling them that they didn't know the Father or have any connection with Him. Jesus' speech is stunning and well worth a read (see John 5:30–47).

So one option is to accept the testimony of God regarding who the Son is. When we accept that testimony, verse 10 says that we then have it within ourselves. John is probably referring here to our union with Christ by the Spirit, as becomes clearer in verses 11–12.

The other option is to reject God's testimony about the Son, which is effectively to declare God to be a liar. In John's Gospel, on average, almost every other sentence Jesus speaks is referencing the Father and the Son. When God spoke from heaven in John 12:28, and earlier at Jesus' baptism, He always spoke of the Son. We simply cannot have the Father without the Son.

So John underlines again the nature of Christianity. God give us eternal life by giving us the Son. Anyone united to Christ is spiritually alive. Anyone not united to Christ is still spiritually dead.

Christianity is not primarily about how we live, or even what we believe. Christianity is primarily about Christ. The wonder of Christianity is that God gave Christ, Christ gave Himself and we get Christ – which means we get everything that Christ has, including His relationship with the Father. Getting that means we have eternal life (John 17:3)!

REFLECTION

How do you see people diminishing Christ and trying to still have life and connection with God the Father? Take the time to give thanks again that the God who saves you is the Trinity.

John wrote this letter to reassure true believers that they were truly saved. They had been on the receiving end of some harsh criticism unhelpfully causing them to feel spiritually inadequate as if they were somehow second-class Christians. John wrote this letter to help them.

When we have confidence that we have eternal life through fellowship with the Trinity, then that confidence will breed further confidence. If I am sure that God loves me and wants fellowship with me, then I am confident that God will listen when I pray. As my desires are aligned with His, then when I speak to Him, I can speak with confidence that He not only hears, but He gives.

The key here is to pray according to His will. This is not a loophole to protect God from having to do the crazy things we might ask. This is a relational reality. God is a giving God as has been proven at the cross. With confidence that His gracious giving nature is aimed in our direction, as we draw close in fellowship we will grow in confidence that what we ask is in line with His values. Consequently as we grow closer to Him, our praying will line up with His values and we know that He will gladly give as we ask (see Rom. 8:32).

Prayer always remains slightly mysterious to us since we might share God's values increasingly, but we never get His perspective fully. Again, this is not about giving God a loophole to avoid answering prayer. It is simply saying that God is not restricted to the extent of our wisdom when we ask. For that we can be thankful!

REFLECTION

How are your values shifting to reflect God's values as you enjoy fellowship with Him? Are you praying with increasing confidence as a result?

Last time we thought about our confidence in asking God for things in prayer. John gives a fitting example of what we might ask. Since the whole letter has been about fellowship with God and loving other people, naturally the example he gives is of asking God something for the sake of someone else.

John identifies the issue of a fellow believer committing a sin. Specifically, he says that this is 'a sin that does not lead to death' (v. 16). Some have created a distinction between forgivable sins and a class of mortal sins. That is not a biblical distinction and John does not have that idea in mind here. In light of all he has written about the Spirit, it is fair to assume that the sin leading to death is the rejection of the Spirit's witness to Jesus. John is instead referring to lesser sins – that is, to everything else. When a fellow member of the community is trapped in a sin, then the brother or sister should pray to God for them and God will give life.

Does this mean that we should not pray for someone who claims to be a Christian, but is rejecting the witness of the Spirit regarding Christ? John is not speaking of that either, but that is not to say we should not pray for their salvation the same as we do for anyone else outside the family of God. Yet we don't pray for them as a brother in Christ.

John's earlier concern about sin in the life of the believer is coming out again here. **As someone who is fellowshipping closely with God, we will share God's concern for family members whose lives are being harmed by sin**. With John we can be confident that a fellow believer's life will not be continuously marred by ongoing sin – so we pray.

REFLECTION

God loves you and every other member of His family that you know. Who can you pray for that is struggling with sin in some way? Pray boldly, for you are praying in line with God's will!

We have arrived at the end of this wonderful letter from John. He ends with a blitz of reality statements to comfort and challenge his readers.

He is confident that he and his readers are from God, but the world around is very much in the power of the evil one. The believers shouldn't be surprised when they face opposition from others, including those who had gone out from the community. The evil one is very much at work and very much opposed to those who are truly in God's family.

To be in God's family is our privilege because the Son of God actually did come into the world. He came on a mission. It was a revelation mission – to give us understanding of who God is. It was a marital mission – to be united with us who are now 'in him'. **Christianity is ultimately wrapped up in our being wrapped up in Christ – we are united to Him**.

What He has done matters profoundly. He has revealed God to us and He has made it possible for us to be united to Himself. Who the Son is matters profoundly. He is the true God and our access to eternal life.

With that reality presented to the readers, John affectionately ends with a warning. 'Dear children,' as has been his tender label for them throughout the letter, 'keep yourselves from idols.' In light of the wonder of being united to Christ by the Spirit and thereby having full access to His Father and ours, in other words in light of the privilege of fellowship with the Trinity, we should avoid going after any other gods. That makes sense. In light of God's love for us why would we want to go anywhere else?

REFLECTION

Take some time to thank God for the privilege of being in the embrace of the Trinity. If you have trusted Christ as your Saviour, then by the Spirit you have Christ as your husband, and His Father as your Father. Fellowship with the Trinity – what better news could there be!

This brief letter is from John to an unnamed lady and her children. It may be that he is writing to a specific lady, perhaps a wealthy lady who hosted a church in her home. It is more likely that he is writing to a local church referred to as a lady, with the members being described as her children.

From the start John ties together the ideas of truth and love. He loves these people 'in the truth' (v. 1), as do others who know the truth. This truth is abiding in us and will be with us forever. Is he referring to the truth of God's Word, or to the Word Incarnate – Jesus Christ, who is 'the way and the truth and the life' (John 14:6)? The answer is probably yes to both. Followers of Jesus are people with truth planted deep within them by the Spirit – the Spirit by whom Christ dwells with and in us forever.

John's opening greeting in verse 3 states that grace, mercy and peace will be with us. For the Christian, these are not words that are nice to hear but empty of meaning. From God we have received grace – the giving of Himself for our sake. We have received mercy – His kindness where we deserved anything but kindness. We have received peace – the order that only God's grace and mercy can bring to a troubled life in an evil world.

How have we received these wonderful blessings from God the Father? John writes that they come from Christ His Son, in truth and love.

In John's Gospel we see that the glory of God is revealed to us in the Son who is 'full of grace and truth' (1:14); that God desires 'worship in spirit and in truth' (4:23–24); that knowing the truth can truly set enslaved people free (8:32–46); that Jesus Himself is the truth (14:6); that the Spirit of truth points people to the Son (15:26); that God's Word is truth (17:17); and that when Pilate stood face to face with the Truth and asked, 'What is truth?' he left before receiving what would have been a fascinating answer (18:37–38)!

All of God's blessings are given to us in the Son in truth and love. It is not truth without love, nor love lacking in truth. God is fully truthful and loving. What a privilege to be on the receiving end of that goodness!

REFLECTION

Does your life demonstrate that you place an equally high value on truth and on love? Ponder how these two work together so perfectly in Christ.

DAY 28

READ 2 John especially verses 4–13

John wrote to this group of believers with both encouraging instruction and helpful warning.

The instruction comes in verses 4–6 and again ties together the concepts of truth and love. These believers were walking in the truth, but they needed to be careful to obey the commandment Jesus gave back in the upper room – to love one another. To obey the commandments of God is to love, since the whole law of God could be summed up by the great command to love God and love neighbour. John is warning against any separation of truth and love. When we love, we fulfil God's greatest command. (Notice in verse 6 that 'commands', in the plural, becomes the singular 'command' by the end of the verse!)

The warning follows in verses 7–11. There are deceivers in the world, people who deny the person and work of Jesus Christ. In that time they were focused on denying that the Son of God really came in the flesh. Today they may seek to undermine the person and work of the Son in other ways. But the spirit driving all such false teaching is satanic. John was concerned that this church would lovingly receive people who weren't abiding in the truth of Christ.

These believers were at risk from an undiscerning love, which might lead them to welcome, host, support and enable false teachers to do further damage to the work of Christ. **The test was to assess how any individuals understood Christ. If they failed that test, even if they claimed to be Christians, they should not be helped or supported in any way**. Such undiscerning love would be the same as participating in their false and wicked works.

As Christians we cannot sacrifice love in the name of truth as some do when their emphasis on their understanding of Christian truth is used to justify a lack of love for others. Equally we cannot sacrifice truth in the name of love as John warned this church in 2 John.

REFLECTION

Pray for God to give you a discerning love for God's work and God's people.

This short letter from John to Gaius is a fascinating insight into the early church. Gaius was in a church being dominated by a man named Diotrephes. Gaius may have hosted the church in his home, and he may or may not have been an elder in the church – we know only what John writes of him. Gaius was loved by John (having perhaps been converted under John's ministry) and he was respected as a man who was walking in the truth. His life lived out his testimony. Gaius was a solid believer.

John prayed that Gaius would be physically healthy as he was spiritually healthy. We often pray for physical health these days, but how often do we fail to pray for spiritual health?

From verses 5–8 we read that Gaius was committed to supporting itinerant ministers of the gospel, and perhaps other believers too. In our time we tend to think of hospitality as being the offer of a meal after church, but in those days it would have included safe lodging as well. The alternatives for travelling Christians were dangerous and difficult, so giving hospitality was a significant ministry for the health of the church at large. By participating through hospitality, Gaius was effectively a fellow worker for the truth.

As we read this personal letter from the apostle to his friend we see something of the inner workings of the church as it spread. **Normal people offered normal homes to help believers who were serving God, and as such became their fellow workers in the truth**.

We live in different times, but hospitality is still such a gift to others. While our culture might assume 'a man's home is his castle' and value personal space, perhaps there are forms of hospitality that would be strategic in the work of the gospel in our time – not only helping ministers and missionaries, but also offering gospel exposure to foreign students, to foster children and even to people looking for real home alternatives to expensive bed and breakfast lodging.

REFLECTION

In what ways are you able to partner in the work of the gospel through hospitality, or through supporting strategic work that others are doing?

John wrote to his friend Gaius and commended him for partnering with gospel workers through the kind gift of hospitality. But this little note is more than a thank you letter. Things were not all happy in this unnamed church community.

Often churches face great difficulties at the hand of an individual. John identifies the problem person in this church – Diotrephes. Again, we don't know much about him. He may or may not have been a leader within the church.

What we do know about Diotrephes is that he liked to put himself first. What a terrible reputation to have! How awful if others were to say that of us, that we like to be first! Diotrephes seems to have been corrupted by a craving for power. Perhaps he was wealthy, or perhaps he was well connected through a network of relatives in the church, or perhaps he had been a strong leader in a time of crisis who now felt indispensable? Whatever the story, his deep flaw of wanting to be first manifested in three behaviours:

1. He refused to submit to genuine authority (v. 9). John was an apostle, but Diotrephes rejected that authority. People with this 'Diotrephes spirit' tend to not like it when others have authority over them.

2. He talked wicked nonsense against John and his associates (v. 10a). Not only did Diotrephes reject the authority of someone who legitimately had authority, but he also sought to undermine that authority by the things he said. The Diotrepheses of our day will tend to betray themselves by their over-zealous and destructive storytelling.

3. He did not love others (v. 10b). Diotrephes did not show love to other believers who were travelling in the area, and he stopped others who were more loving than he was. The attitude of individuals like Diotrephes will always be to seek to squelch the love in others as well as failing to be loving themselves.

Churches can be crippled by power-hungry and unloving people like Diotrephes. Often these individuals will gain positions of power and wield their unappreciated and ungodly authority over others. John was ready to deal with Diotrephes, but this is never an easy step to take for a church. For the health of the church, however, humble and godly discipline needs to protect the flock and the witness of the church from men like this.

REFLECTION

Does your church have a Diotrephes at work in it? Pray and ask God to give you wisdom about what to do. Or are you a Diotrephes? Get help.

In this personal letter to Gaius we read John expressing support for the loving and generous Gaius. We also read his condemnation of the troublesome Diotrephes. Finally he gives a glowing recommendation for a man named Demetrius.

John urges Gaius not to fall into the trap of playing Diotrephes' game – that is, he is not to imitate evil, but to continue to imitate good. It is tempting when there is a Diotrephes loose in the church to start to act like that person. After all, they seem to have such influence, and will typically be able to rationalise and justify the way they work. John tries to point the gaze of Gaius away from this man, however.

The good alternative that he offers is a man named Demetrius. This individual, again one we know very little about, has a glowing reference from John. He was spoken well of by everyone, 'and even by the truth itself' (v. 12). This almost certainly meant that **Demetrius so lived out what the Scripture teaches that the Scriptures ended up functioning as an endorsement of him**. John then adds his own testimony in support of that.

There are a couple of key lessons to ponder here:

1. Who are we imitating? Forceful characters will tend to get our attention, but not every forceful character is a godly example to follow. Beware that in the church there will be people whose attitude, methods and character are deeply flawed. Beware of people who talk a good game, but actually compromise what they may claim by how they act. Beware of any that are eager to be pre-eminent in a church. Beware of any that are power hungry. Instead look for men and women of godly character, like Demetrius, and imitate them.

2. How is our reputation? We should not be living to gain reputation, but we do have one. Surely our desire is to live our lives in response to God, in line with the truth, so that like Demetrius the truth can give a good testimony of our lives. This is not a matter of effort or pretence. This is a matter of character being shaped by God so that we are like Him.

REFLECTION

Pray and ask God for good examples to imitate in others, and for God to make you the kind of person that others should also imitate.

MORE IN THIS SERIES

ROMANS
Momentous News
By David Cook
ISBN: 978-1-906173-24-1

MARK
The Suffering Servant
By Jeremy McQuoid
ISBN: 978-1-906173-55-5

DANIEL
Far From Home
By Justin Mote
ISBN: 978-1-906173-68-5

1 THESSALONIANS
Living for Jesus
By Julia Marsden
ISBN: 978-1-906173-67-8

PHILIPPIANS
Press Towards the Goal
By Kay Mumford
ISBN: 978-1-909611-31-3

GALATIANS
The Life I Now Live
By Peter Mead
ISBN: 978-1-910587-09-6

ACTS
To the Ends of the Earth
By David Cook
ISBN: 978-1-909611-02-3

EZEKIEL
For His Glory
By Peter Lau
ISBN: 978-1-909611-83-2

JOHN
Never Thirst Again
By David Cook
ISBN: 978-1-909611-30-6

and more at...  **10** Publishing
a division of **10** ofthose.com

To place an order call: **0330 2233 423** email: **sales@10ofthose.com**
or order online: **www.10ofthose.com**

a division of **10** ofthose.com

10Publishing is the publishing house of **10ofThose**. It is committed to producing quality Christian resources that are biblical and accessible.

www.10ofthose.com is our online retail arm selling thousands of quality books at discounted prices.

For information contact: **sales@10ofthose.com** or check out our website: **www.10ofthose.com**